Just Dance

Dance Team

Candice Ransom
and Madeline Nixon

AV2

www.av2books.com

Step 1
Go to **www.av2books.com**

Step 2
Enter this unique code

ZKBOWIS8X

Step 3
Explore your interactive eBook!

AV2 is optimized for use on any device

Your interactive eBook comes with...

Contents
Browse a live contents page to easily navigate through resources

Audio
Listen to sections of the book read aloud

Videos
Watch informative video clips

Weblinks
Gain additional information for research

Try This!
Complete activities and hands-on experiments

Key Words
Study vocabulary, and complete a matching word activity

Quizzes
Test your knowledge

Slideshows
View images and captions

... and much, much more!

Dance Team

Contents

Dance teams are popular at sporting events.

Chapter 1

Ready, Set, Dance!

It is halftime at the football game. The crowd goes quiet. Onto the field marches the dance team!

There are two types of dance teams. **Kickline** dance teams are noted for their high kicks. Each kick is performed in **unison**. Jazz dance teams mostly use jazz dance **techniques**. Sometimes, a dance team will perform both styles. Either way, dance teams know how to entertain a crowd.

Dance teams grew from other activities. Cheerleading teams, drill teams, and pep squads all entertain fans at school games. The first cheerleaders yelled chants at football games. Drill teams march in patterns. Pep squads lead cheers, often using **pom-poms**.

Dance teams sometimes
perform with pom-poms.

The Kilgore College Rangerettes have gone on several world tours in their 70 plus years of existence.

Dance teams share features with those activities. The main difference is that dance teams dance.

In 1929, the first dancing pep squad performed in Texas. Then came the Rangerettes in 1940. The all-girl team danced and kicked across the Kilgore College football field in Texas. Other schools also formed dance teams. In 1968, the first dance team **competition** was held in California. Today, dance teams compete all over the world.

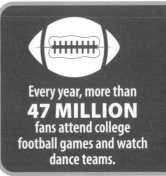

Every year, more than **47 MILLION** fans attend college football games and watch dance teams.

The **BEST** college dance team in the United States is the University of Nevada Rebel Girls.

Dance Team Timeline

Dance teams first formed in high school and college settings. Teams like this still exist, but they have evolved. Dance teams also perform in entertainment shows, parades, and **professional** sporting events.

1925

The Rockettes, a precision kickline dance team, are established in St. Louis. Since 1932, they have performed at Radio City Music Hall.

1929

Gussie Nell Davis establishes the Flaming Flashes and later, the Kilgore College Rangerettes.

1936

Kay Teer forms a group of 50 women at Edinburg High School in Texas to perform at high school football games. The dance team is known as the Red and Blue Sergeanettes.

The Kilgore Rangerettes

There are several dance team levels, including youth, college, all-star, and professional.

1940s

Pep squads and drill teams develop across the United States in order to boost happiness and morale during World War II.

1968

The first dance team competition is held in California.

Today

Dance teams are more popular than ever. They can be found in colleges around the world. International dance team competitions are held annually.

Chapter 2

Fancy Feet

Flexible clothes are important for dance teams. Dancers usually practice in leggings. Having the right dancing shoes is also key. Sometimes tennis shoes work well. However, both kickline and jazz dance teams can wear slip-on jazz dance shoes.

Dance teams rehearse in clothing that makes it easy to move around.

The real fun comes at showtime. Team members that perform at sporting events wear matching uniforms. Jazz dance team members might wear glittery costumes with short skirts. Kickline dance teams might wear shorts or tights and a fancy top.

Dance teams usually perform in slip-on jazz dance shoes or character shoes. Character shoes have high heels. They also have straps across the feet.

Dance Tip

Dancing requires flexibility. Always warm and stretch your muscles before a class or performance.

High school and college dance teams wear the same uniforms to promote the school's identity.

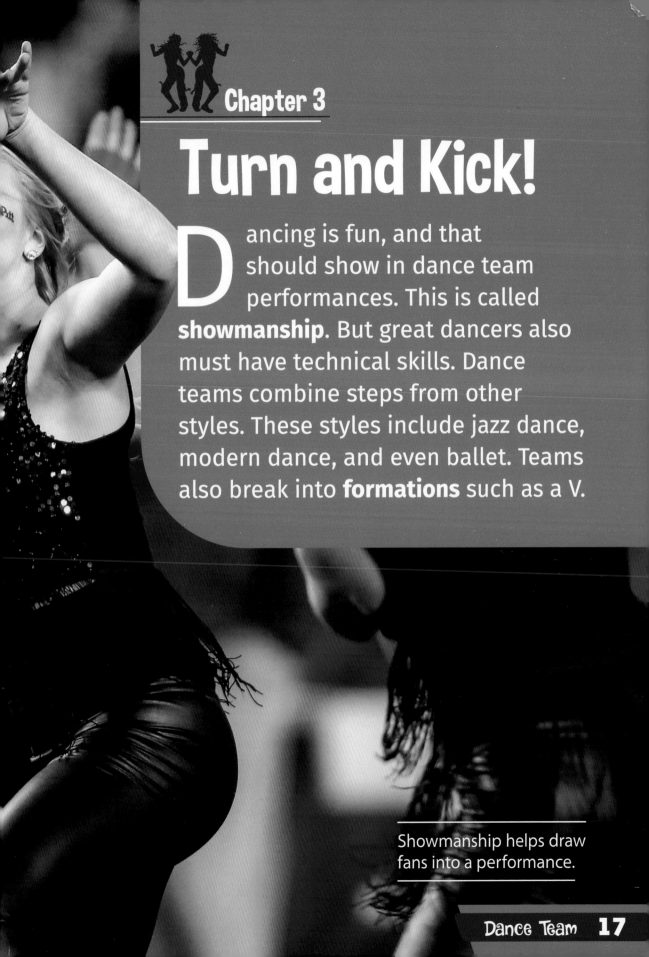

Chapter 3

Turn and Kick!

Dancing is fun, and that should show in dance team performances. This is called **showmanship**. But great dancers also must have technical skills. Dance teams combine steps from other styles. These styles include jazz dance, modern dance, and even ballet. Teams also break into **formations** such as a V.

Showmanship helps draw fans into a performance.

Dancers are always moving. They may move as one or they may have individual **choreography**. Sometimes, they work together as a group. This shows during pirouettes. Those are complete turns done on one foot. Each member of the dance team turns at the same time. The audience watches the entire team, not a single dancer.

Dance Tip

When you dance, lift your chin and look straight ahead. Do not look at the floor or your feet.

It takes a lot of practice for everyone to pirouette and kick at the exact same time.

The Radio City Rockettes are known for their kicklines.

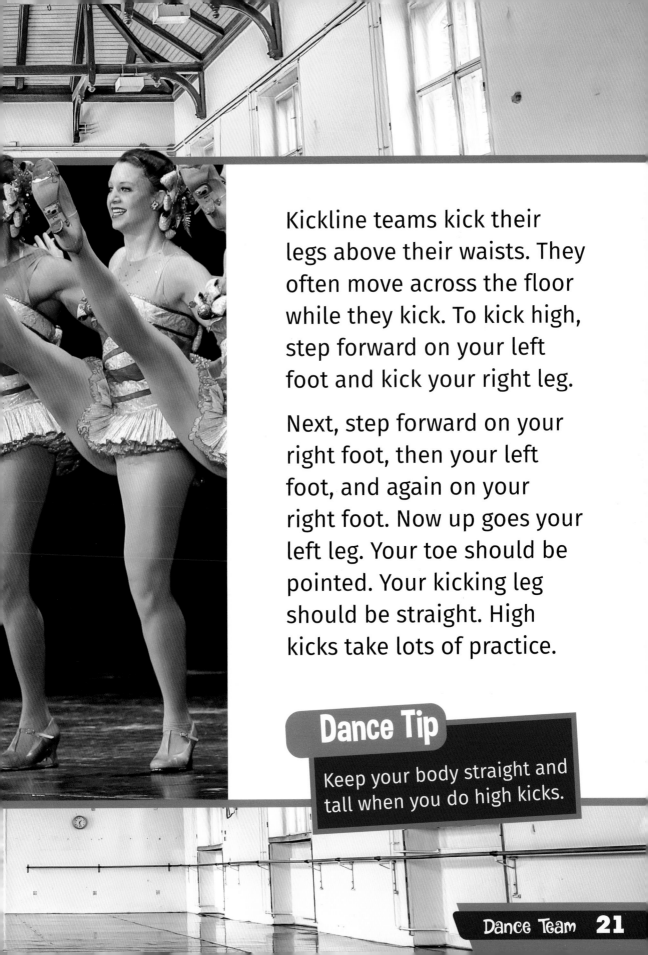

Kickline teams kick their legs above their waists. They often move across the floor while they kick. To kick high, step forward on your left foot and kick your right leg.

Next, step forward on your right foot, then your left foot, and again on your right foot. Now up goes your left leg. Your toe should be pointed. Your kicking leg should be straight. High kicks take lots of practice.

Dance Tip

Keep your body straight and tall when you do high kicks.

Fan Kick

Both jazz and kickline dance teams perform fan kicks. You can practice these at home.

1. To do a right kick, brush out with your right foot. Point your right toes toward the left corner of the room.

2. Kick your right leg upward. It should go toward the left corner of the room.

3. Swing your right leg in a half-circle. The motion should look like the shape of a fan. Your toes end pointed toward the right corner of the room.

4. Brush your feet back together and step down on your right foot.

College dancers perform at basketball and football games.

Chapter 4

Dance Team Dreams

Dance teams borrow movements from other dance styles. That is why dance team members often take classes in styles such as jazz, modern dance, and ballet. Some even take gymnastics lessons. Routines might require floor splits or **cartwheels**. Classes help dancers learn these techniques.

The summer is an important time for dance teams. Sometimes, dancers go to camps. They work on their skills there. They also learn new routines.

The fun really begins in the fall. That is when school begins. Dance teams often perform at sporting events. Sometimes, they perform in pep rallies, too.

College dance teams usually practice **4 DAYS** a week for **2 HOURS**.

A kickline routine must have a **MINIMUM** of **50 KICKS**.

Dance teams can help inspire school spirit.

Dance teams also compete. Teams from different schools come together. Each team performs. Then, judges score the performances.

The judges look at different things. They judge the difficulty of turns and jumps. They count the number of kicks in a kickline routine. They also judge if teams are performing as one. Whoever has the highest score wins. Some teams travel all over the United States to compete.

Dance team is about more than competition, though. It is about spending time with your friends. It is about performing in front of your classmates. And it is about having a great time dancing to fun music!

Dance Tip

Never wear your dance shoes on the street. Rough sidewalks can scratch the smooth leather soles.

Dancers work hard to entertain the crowd and win competitions.

Quiz

1 What was the name of the first college dance team?

2 What is the minimum number of kicks in a kickline routine?

3 What styles of dance might a dance team incorporate?

4 Where do the Rockettes perform?

5 What do some dance team members do in the summer?

6 What are character shoes?

7 What might a jazz dance team wear?

8 What is just as important as technical skills?

9 Where was the first dance team competition?

10 What activities did dance teams grow from?

Key Words

cartwheels tumbling moves in which dancers do sideways handsprings

choreography dance steps or routines that a dancer has created

competition an event in which teams try to beat each other

formations arrangements of people in groups

kickline a type of dance team in which dancers in a line kick at the same time

pom-poms fluffy balls held by cheerleaders

professional a person who makes a living in a certain field

showmanship the ability to perform in a theatrical way

techniques skills used in physical movements, such as dance

unison at the same time

Index

Get the best of both worlds.

AV2 bridges the gap between print and digital.

The expandable resources toolbar enables quick access to content including **videos**, **audio**, **activities**, **weblinks**, **slideshows**, **quizzes**, and **key words**.

Animated videos make static images come alive.

Resource icons on each page help readers to further **explore key concepts**.

Published by AV2
350 5th Avenue, 59th Floor
New York, NY 10118
Website: www.av2books.com

Library of Congress Cataloging-in-Publication Data
Names: Ransom, Candice F., 1952- author.
Title: Dance team / Candice Ransom and Madeline Nixon.
Description: New York, NY : AV2, 2021. | Series: Just dance | Includes
   index. | Audience: Ages 8-12 | Audience: Grades 4-6
Identifiers: LCCN 2020000744 (print) | LCCN 2020000745 (ebook) | ISBN
   9781791123161 (library binding) | ISBN 9781791123178 (paperback) | ISBN
   9781791123185 | ISBN 9781791123192
Subjects: LCSH: Dance--Juvenile literature. | Dance teams--Juvenile
   literature.
Classification: LCC GV1798 .R13 2021 (print) | LCC GV1798 (ebook) | DDC
   793.3--dc23
LC record available at https://lccn.loc.gov/2020000744
LC ebook record available at https://lccn.loc.gov/2020000745

Printed in Guangzhou, China
1 2 3 4 5 6 7 8 9 0 24 23 22 21 20

022020
101119

Project Coordinator: Heather Kissock   Designer: Ana María Vidal

Every reasonable effort has been made to trace ownership and to obtain permission to reprint copyright material. The publishers would be pleased to have any errors or omissions brought to their attention so that they may be corrected in subsequent printings.

Weigl acknowledges Getty Images, Alamy, Newscom, iStock, and Shutterstock as its primary image suppliers for this title.

First published by North Star Editions in 2018.